Learn French

A Fast and Easy Guide for Beginners to Learn Conversational French

Free membership into the Mastermind Self Development Group!

For a limited time, you can join the Mastermind Self Development Group for free! You will receive videos and articles from top authorities in self development as well as a special group only offers on new books and training programs. There will also be a monthly member only draw that gives you a chance to win any book from your Kindle wish list!

If you sign up through this link http://www.mastermindselfdevelopment.com/specialreport you will also get a special free report on the Wheel of Life. This report will give you a visual look at your current life and then take you through a series of exercises that will help you plan what your perfect life looks like. The workbook does not end there; we then take you through a process to help you plan how to achieve that perfect life. The process is very powerful and has the potential to change your life forever. Join the group now and start to change your life!
http://www.mastermindselfdevelopment.com/specialreport

Table of Contents

Introduction

Chapter 1: French - how does it work?

Chapter 2: Pronunciation

Chapter 3: Past and Future Tenses

Chapter 4: Questions and Objects

Chapter 5: Adjectives, Adverbs, Conjunctions, and Prepositions

Chapter 6: Conversational Necessities

Conclusion

© Copyright 2016 by Mastermind Self Development All rights reserved.

The follow eBook is reproduced below with the goal of providing information that is as accurate and reliable as possible. Regardless, purchasing this eBook can be seen as consent to the fact that both the publisher and the author of this book are in no way experts on the topics discussed within and that any recommendations or suggestions that are made herein are for entertainment purposes only. Professionals should be consulted as needed prior to undertaking any of the action endorsed herein.

This declaration is deemed fair and valid by both the American Bar Association and the Committee of Publishers Association and is legally binding throughout the United States.

Furthermore, the transmission, duplication or reproduction of any of the following work including specific information will be considered an illegal act irrespective of if it is done electronically or in print. This extends to creating a secondary or tertiary copy of the work or a recorded copy and is only allowed with express written consent from the Publisher. All additional right reserved.

The information in the following pages is broadly considered to be a truthful and accurate account of facts and as such any inattention, use or misuse of the information in question by the reader will render any resulting actions solely under their purview. There are no scenarios in which the publisher or the original author of this work can be in any fashion deemed liable for any hardship or damages that may befall them after undertaking information described herein.

Additionally, the information in the following pages is intended only for informational purposes and should thus be thought of as universal. As befitting its nature, it is presented without assurance regarding its prolonged validity or interim quality. Trademarks that are mentioned are done without written consent and can in no way be considered an endorsement from the trademark holder.

Introduction

Congratulations on downloading **Learn French** and thank you for doing so.

The following chapters will discuss what is in my opinion the best and most efficient way to learn the French language.

If you're reading this, it's of course because you have an interest in learning French. There are many reasons that you may have such an interest. Maybe you've gotten a job offer which would require you to relocate to Québec or France or Morocco. Maybe you're having a hard time keeping up with your college or high school French classes and looking for some extracurricular guidance. Maybe it's just for the pure purpose of leisure and you don't really have any additional motives.

Regardless of what your goal ultimately is, my goal is to help you meet it. Throughout the course of this book, you're going to be learning quite a lot of things regarding French. In the first chapter, we'll be covering the bare essentials of sentence structure and verbiage, as well as covering essential differences between French and English. In the second, we're going to be talking more about the precise pronunciation rules of French. In the third, we're going to be talking about the past and future tenses. The fourth is going to be talking more about direct and indirect object pronouns. The fifth chapter is going to discuss higher end grammatical concepts. The fifth chapter is going to discuss basic French conversation and give you some useful phrases for travel.

There are plenty of books on this subject on the market, thanks again for choosing this one! Every effort was made to ensure it is full of as much useful information as possible, please enjoy!

Chapter 1: French - how does it work?

So many people all the time everywhere make an extreme error in learning languages: they fail to look at it in the context óf a *language* and instead try to turn it into a game of memorization. This doesn't work. There are good and bad ways to learn language, and if at the end of the day, all you have to show for yourself are a few phrases memorized off of some flash cards, then frankly, you're learning the language in a bad way.

I've been trying to communicate how to learn languages for a very long time and I'm still having a hard time determining whether I think language learning is an art or a science. Regardless, the truth is that there is no one perfect way to learn a language, because we all learn in terribly different ways, which makes it nigh impossible to pin down one singular way which would most work.

However, there are certain natural mechanisms for picking up languages that people of average intelligence and greater can utilize in order to pick up language really easily.

We don't come out of the womb learning a language. We come out as a blank slate. We have the *ability* to speak language, but it's unformed; a baby born in China will learn a form of Chinese, and a baby born in England will learn English.

Babies can't read flash cards. And while our natural propensity to learn a language demonstrably goes down as a person ages, there are numerous reasons for this which aren't normally accounted for.

A child has to learn a language in order to survive and communicate, and has an easy time learning a language due to the fact that it's completely immersed in it.

There are language learning gurus out there who are polyglots because they put themselves in similar situations in order to learn language: the immerse themselves near entirely in the language by traveling from place to place and making it so that they have to speak and understand the language to survive and communicate.

Now, it's likely not feasible for you to up and relocate to Quebec or France just in order to learn a language. But that's not to say that we can't trigger the same sort of intuitive language learning processes that these language learning gurus and these children are tapping into.

In other words, this entire method is based around the idea that if you have the proper springboard and the proper background, you can do any number of things with the language that you wish simply by natural self guided immersion and active effort in learning the language.

My goal in this book isn't to give you a vocabulary list to memorize, nor is it to give you a precise grammatical explanation of every single thing (though I'll certainly try to give accurate and succinct explanations), but rather it's to help you streamline the natural language learning processes so that you don't, well, forget every last thing that you learn in the process of reading this book.

The way that they taught you to learn languages in high school was wrong. Cut and dry, 100%, it was not the right way to go about it. Well, it was and it wasn't. It was right in some capacities - you likely had to listen to and repeat phrases in the class, which was solid basic immersion. But the idea of regurgitating vocab words onto a test is bizarre and ludicrous and just a way to ensure that you forget the very words you learned the following year.

The only way to avoid this sort of situation is by actively using the vocabulary and words that you've learned, but the reality is that a lot of high schools - especially ones with less funding - don't try particularly hard with their pen pal projects or anything of that nature.

Anyhow, the purpose of this book is to *streamline* the process of learning a language intuitively. There are a few different ways in which I'm going to try earnestly to do this. The first is by explaining the *differences* between English and French.

You may be wondering, "why would you do that? Why not start with the similarities?"

Well, the simple answer is because any language has more happening in common with another language than it has happening differently. This may sound bizarre, but think about it - every language is just a form of communication. There are various differences between them but ultimately they're all attempting to accomplish the same essential key concept: the usage of verbal cues in order to denote or tell a given thing.

However, for all the similarities, languages can also be incredibly *different*. For example, if I were going to try to tell the similarities between English and Japanese, the list would be incredibly short, by mere virtue of the fact that English and Japanese have little truly in common. Grammatically, they are incredibly different beasts. On top of this, the vocabulary is very different. It's much easier to make you understand the ways in which Japanese and English *are* different than try to expect you to latch onto the things that are.

When you're told things that are similar between languages, you latch onto those concepts. You're unaware of the vast amount of differences and you may, in fact, make very simple mistakes. One common such mistake in French is the combination of the existence and state verb *être* with the present participle of another verb.

In English, we use this to construct the present continuous tense. For example:

I *am eating*.

He *is playing*.

They *are walking*.

However, this isn't such the case in French. The equivalent phrases would be along the lines of:

Je *suis mangant*.

Il *est jouant*.

Ils *sont marchant*.

But this isn't correct at all, and in fact sound particularly bizarre and out of place to other French speakers. The correct way would be to conjugate the infinitive of the directly referenced verb (to eat, to play, to walk) for the present indicative and completely leave the *être* (to be) verb out of it:

Je *mange*.

Il *joue*.

Ils *marchent*.

There are a great number of differences between English and French as such that you'll somewhat naturally pick up as we go along, but that I'll point out regardless.

We'll be getting a lot more into the exact pronunciation of the given sounds in French in the next chapter, but for right now, I just want to give you some phrases and verbs that you can work with *as we speak*. Throughout this book, I'm going to be giving you pronunciation guides where possible. Some sounds are hard to approximate without using a phonetic alphabet, however.

One particular sound is the sound made in "je" and "le" and similar words. You may be tempted, especially if you have experience in other Romance languages where the sounds are very cut and dry, to pronounce these as "jeh" and "leh", as in "JEffrey" or "LEt's go", but you can't do that. This sound is actually much closer to the *oo* sound in *book* (U.S. English).

For phonetic purposes, this specific sound will be represented with the letters *uu*.

It's also important to bear in mind going forward that every *r* in Modern French is pronounced in a very guttural trill, quite similar to the German *r*, though not quite as intense. (though it's particularly hard for a language to be anywhere near as intense as German is, truthfully.) The only exception is generally in rural communities in Quebec or among the elderly in Southern France. Otherwise, the sound is guttural and produced from airflow at the back of the throat. It can be difficult to ascertain at first, but you can find YouTube videos concerning the French *r* to help you to understand it.

So if I were to write the following phrase:

Je prends un sandwich. *(I'll take/have a sandwich.)*

I would write the pronunciation for it as such:

juu PRAHND uh(n) sand-WEECH

The *n* in parentheses denotes that the consonant should be barely uttered and heard. This is a scale which takes practice, and plays into a major part of French pronunciation, as we'll cover in the next chapter. For now, just follow my pronunciation text, because French pronunciation is an independent fish to fry that I don't want to tackle in this chapter.

There are still more differences between French and English, and it's really important to bear these in mind as you go forward, too.

First off, they are not pronounced similarly, at all. There will be several cognates that you'll run into that look quite similar to the English phrase but are pronounced nothing the same. Take, for example, the word "horrible". In French, the *h* is silent, the *r* would be guttural, and the *ble* consonant, which would sound like "bull" in English, sounds like "bluu" in French. So we go from *HOR-ih-bull* to *or-EEH-bluu*. *Il y a un grand différence entre les deux!* (There's a big difference between the two!)

That's not even including *false cognates* which you need to be incredibly wary of. Take for instance the word *terrible*. It also exists in French, where in a literary sense, it means something very similar to the English "terrible". However, if you were to ask a French person how they're doing, and they said "*pas terrible*", you may think they're saying "not bad" or "not terrible", but this isn't the case. In fact, *terrible* (tuu-REEH-bluu) in the colloquial sense means "great". So "*pas terrible*" really means "not great" or "not the best".

Going beyond that, a lot of things are somewhat topsy turvy in French. Take the phrase "*yaourt aux fruits*". This means "yogurt with fruit". However, "*aux*" is a contraction of "à les", meaning "to the" or "at the". The typical French word for "with" would indeed be "*avec*", as in "*Je vais aller au MGC avec mes copains*" ("I'm going to the mall with my friends."). However, "with" doesn't have as many uses in French as it does in English, and to express the innate quality of something, or the idea of something belonging to something else in a categorical sense, you use à rather than avec.

One last super important difference that we're going to cover at this given moment is saying your occupation. In English, we say "I am *a professor*" or "I am *a butcher*". However, the French leave this article out. To them, an occupation is an intrinsic quality, which somewhat makes sense if you think about it. So instead of saying "*Je suis un professeur*" (I am a professor), the French would rather say

"*Je suis professeur*" (literally 'I am professor').

Basic sentence structure

Anyhow, let's get to the meat of this chapter, because there's still quite a bit left to cover: subjects and verbs. This is the basis of every single sentence we speak. I'm sure that, by now, you know what a subject is. A *subject* is the word which denotes the performer of an action.

My dog **is** big.

In this sentence, *my dog* is the subject, where **is** is the verb (to be). Every language has a specific order in which they put subjects, objects, and verbs (an object being the *direct recipient* of an action, such as "*I* **love** cats", where "cats" is the object).

Subject pronouns

In English, we use sentence pronouns quite often. In fact, we use them in nearly every sentence!

Just to prove it, I'm going to type those two sentences again and underline the subject pronouns.

In English, we use sentence pronouns quite often. In fact, we use them in nearly every sentence!

So what is a sentence pronoun? A sentence pronoun is anything which replaces giving the direct name of something in the sentence. Take for example the sentence "John plays basketball."

Normally, if we've already brought John up as the topic of conversation, we can contextually replace his name and still have it be clear that we're talking about him specifically. We would do this by saying "he plays basketball."

Then, we use *we, I,* and *you* per standard, because there's not really a first or second direct *noun*. All direct nouns are by their nature in the third person. If your name were Janet, and you were asking me for directions, I wouldn't say "Janet needs to go to the light and turn left." The *you* would imply that I'm speaking *directly* to you, and the fact that I'm talking to you directly conversely implies that I need to use *you* in the first place, because the fact that I'm talking directly *to* someone and not directly *of* someone puts the sentence in the second person. Thus, I would say "You need to go to the light and turn left."

In English, we have several different subject pronouns. However, we still have less than French, miraculously.

Here are the ones that we mainly use in English:

I - first person singular.

you	-	second person singular.
He, she, it	-	third person singular
we	-	first person plural
they	-	third person plural

French, likewise, has numerous. They also have something we don't: a second person plural. We do have them, but they're informal and unstandardized. For example, in the Southern U.S. you may hear "y'all", and up north and in Britain you'll often hear "you guys". However, we don't have a singular word to refer to multiple people, and they do.

They also have the concept of *formality*. This means that in the second person singular formation, they will use different words depending entirely upon who they're talking to. For example, if you're talking to somebody you just met, someone older than you, or someone in a position of authority over you, you will always use the formal second-person pronoun, which coincidentally is also the second person plural. You use the informal second-person form, the equivalent of English "you" and German "du", when you're around people younger than you, family members, or people that you have met more than once.

The French pronouns are as follows:

Je (juu)	-	first person singular
Tu (too)	-	second person singular
Il/elle (il/el)	-	third person singular
Nous (noo)	-	first person plural
Vous (voo) formal	-	second person plural / first person singular
Ils/elles (il/el) *elles* for females	-	third person plural, *ils* for males/mixed gender,

If you haven't figured it out, in French, you nearly never say the last syllable. The only case in which you do is if it's followed by a vowel, and even then, there are a lot of exceptions. You'll pick up on this a lot more as you actually work with the language and discover the parameters and tendencies of it. We'll talk more about the difference between *ils* and *elles* momentarily.

On

On is a super important term in French that you're going to run into a lot. It has a direct translation to the English *one*.

When talking to a boss, one says "vous".

Quand parler au patron, on dit << vous >>.

However, it also has an implicit meaning of "we" in reference to an unspecific group.

In France, we drink wine.

En France, on boit le vin.

What's more, in colloquial French, people will often use *on* instead of *nous* in order to avoid the more verbose nous conjugations. Compare the following sentences which mean *we're going to go to the movies*:

On va aller au cinéma. (ohn va AL-ley oh seen-ey-mah, in practice the *va* and *aller* sound like one word: ohn v'AL-ley oh seen-ey-mah)

Nous allons aller au cinéma. (nooz AL-lohn AL-ley oh seen-ey-mah)

The first is much easier to say and remember. This will become far more obvious the more that you work with French and get to more complex conjugations, such as the imperfect tense.

This pronoun deserved its own place because it's very unique and doesn't quite have a direct approximate in English. It is *always* conjugated like the *il/elle* third person pronouns, as it's a third person pronoun itself.

Verb conjugation

Verbs are always conjugated in one way or another. However, English actually has one of the easiest verb conjugation systems of any language. The only thing which makes English verb conjugation particularly difficult is the tendency of it to be irregular and for there to be a lot of verbs to cover terribly specific situations. For example, take the phrase "to wait for". You would think, given the commonness of this particular verb and situation, it would be a verb of its own accord. However, this isn't the case. French, however, *does* have a verb for this - *attendre*. "J'attends mes amis." corresponds to "I'm waiting for my friends."

Anyway, English's verb conjugation is indeed rather simple. However, it still exists in some ways. The normal way that we conjugate regular verbs is to, in the raw indicative form, to add an -s to the third person singular. Like so:

I *eat*, you *eat*, he/she/it *eat**s***, we *eat*, they *eat*.

Or, if it's a present continuous verb, we'll use the auxiliary verb "to be" (which is irregular) before the gerund of the given verb, as we talked about earlier:

I *am eating*, you *are eating*, he/she/it *is eating*, we *are eating*, they *are eating*.

French has a more nuanced system of conjugation than English. There are more endings and forms and even tenses. The saving grace, however, is they tend to follow a pattern all on their own. Once you learn this pattern, verbs become far easier.

The present indicative and the present continuous form a singular tense in French, known simply as the *présent*, which of course means "present". The present can be conjugated in many ways but tends to follow a pattern, as you'll see momentarily.

There are three categories of French verbs: *-re* verbs, *-er* verbs, and *-ir* verbs. Most verbs are *regular*, which means that they follow specific patterns of usage and spelling. There is some contention here, in that quite a few verbs are *irregular*... including the ones which are arguably the most common.

That's not to discourage you at all, though, as even the irregular verbs follow a very similar pattern to the regular verbs. So without further ado, let's conjugate some verbs!

First, we're going to focus on *-er* verbs, with the specific example of *parler*, meaning "to speak".

Parler - *to speak*

Conjugation	Meaning	Pronunciation
Je parl*e*	I speak	Juu pahrl
Tu parl*es*	You speak	Too pahrl
Il/elle/on parl*e*	He/she/it/one speaks	Il/el/ohn pahrl
Nous parl*ons*	We speak	Noo pahr-lohn
Vous parl*ez*	You all/you (f.) speak	Voo pahr-ley
Ils/elles parl*ent*	They speak	Il/el pahrl

The way that conjugation works is by dropping the final two letters of the regular verb, always -er, -ir-, or -re, and replacing them with the given suffix. The suffixes for each pronoun are italicized.

As you can see, the endings for *-er* verbs are *-e*, *-es*, *-e*, *-ons*, *-ez*, and *-ent*.

Now is a better time than any to make a mental note for you: you do NOT pronounce the *-ent* suffix on *-er* verbs. Ever. The verb sounds functionally the same as the third person *singular* conjugation.

Anyway, now let's do an *-ir* verb. The endings for *-ir* verbs are *-is*, *-is*, *-it*, *-issons*, *-issez*, and *-issent*. You don't pronounce the *-ent* here, either. However, it doesn't sound like the third person singular, because the third person singular ends in a *t* sound (if followed by a vowel) or none at all, where the third person plural ends in an *s* sound.

Finir - *to finish*

Conjugation	Meaning	Pronunciation
Je fin*is*	I finish	Juu fee-nee
Tu fin*is*	You finish	Too fee-nee
Il/elle/on fin*it*	He/she/it/one finishes	Il/el/ohn fee-nee
Nous fin*issons*	We finish	Noo fee-nee-sohn
Vous fin*issez*	You all/you (f.) finish	Voo fee-nee-sey
Ils/elles fin*issent*	They finish	Il/el fee-nees

And lastly, we're going to work with regular -re verbs. -Re verbs can be somewhat tricky, because they change the scheme up a bit. The third person singular doesn't add *anything* to the stem. Thus, the -re verb endings are as follows: -s, -s, nothing, -ons, -ez, -ent. Let's practice this using the verb *vendre*, meaning "to sell".

Vendre - *to sell*

Conjugation	Meaning	Pronunciation
Je vend*s*	I sell	Juu vahnd
Tu vend*s*	You sell	Too vahnd
Il/elle/on vend	He/she/it/one sells	Il/el/ohn vahn
Nous vend*ons*	We sell	Noo vahnd-ohns
Vous vend*ez*	You all/you (f.) sell	Voo vahnd-ey
Ils/elles vend*ent*	They sell	Il/el vahnd

Do you see how this is working? These verbs all follow a very certain manner of spelling, but it certainly does have an order that you can really easily pick up on. And if it seems difficult now, don't worry - it will most definitely make more sense with practice.

I'd like to move onto articles, but we can't quite yet. This is because we need to cover some major *irregular* verbs. These are verbs that you may use which don't follow the same rules as the verbs prior. These are verbs that you'll learn with practice. The first one that we're going to cover is "to be", or *être*. Here's how you conjugate it.

Être - *to be*

Conjugation	Meaning	Pronunciation
Je suis	I am	Juu swee
Tu es	You are	Too ey
Il/elle/on est	He/she/it/one is	Il/el/ohn ey
Nous sommes	We are	Noo sohm
Vous êtes	You all/you (f.) are	Vooz eht
Ils/elles sont	They are	Il/el sohn

You use être pretty much as you would expect to use it. There are certain places where the translation of "to be" don't quite work across English to French, though, but we'll get there in a second.

You use être in order to describe something or somebody, as well as to tell where you are. It actually corresponds largely to "to be" in English, but there are certain cases where it does. For example, in English, we'd say "I'm 20 years old". *Mais en français*, we'd say "I have 20 years". There are a few other examples I'll list off momentarily, after going into the conjugation of "to have".

Avoir - *to have*

Conjugation	Meaning	Pronunciation
J'ai (*Je ai* contraction)	I have	Jey
Tu as	You have	Too ah
Il/elle/on a	He/she/it/one has	Il/el/ohn ah
Nous av*ons*	We have	Noo ah-vohn
Vous av*ez*	You all/you (f.) have	Voo ah-vey
Ils/elles ont	They have	Il/el ohn

So to say *I'm twenty years old* in French, you'd say *j'ai vingt ans* (jey VAHNT ahn) - "I have twenty years".

There are some embarrassing mix-ups between être and avoir which might happen. You need to be mindful and aware of these. Consider, for example, the sentence "I am full". You might be tempted to translate this directly: *je suis plein*. But this is a HORRIBLE idea! Why? Because "*Je suis plein*" *does* mean "I'm full"... as in "I'm full with a baby."

Instead, you'd say ***J'ai*** *plein*, or roughly "I have fullness".

This likewise plays out with "I'm hot". If you were to say "Je suis chaude" as a woman, you'd be telling somebody you're *aroused*. Rather, you'd want to say "J'ai chaude" - "I have hot". This means that the temperature is hot, or that you feel an uncomfortable heat.

Avoir is used for a few other phrases similarly to describe personal feelings. *J'ai faim* would mean "I'm hungry", though it literally means *I have hunger*.

The next verb we have to cover is *faire*. *Faire* technically means "to do" or "to make", but it has a ton of idiomatic expressions as well. Here's how you conjugate faire:

Faire - *to do, to make*

Conjugation	Meaning	Pronunciation
Je fais	I do, I make	Juu feh
Tu fais	You do, you make	Too feh
Il/elle/on fait	He/she/it/one does, he/she/it/one makes	Il/el/ohn feh
Nous fais*ons*	We do, we make	Noo feh-zohn
Vous faites	You all/you (f.) do, you all/you (f.) make	Voo feht
Ils/elles font	They do, they make	Il/el fohn

There are many cases where you'll use "faire", like so.

Où est Timothie? (Where is Timothy?)

*Dans sa chambre. Il **fait** <u>ses devoirs</u>.* (He's in his room. He's *doing* **his homework**.)

It's also has quite a few idiomatic uses. For example, if it's a nice day out, you would say "*Il fait beau*" - literally "It's doing handsome". If it's hot, you'd say "*il fait chaud*" and if it's cold, you'd say "*il fait froid*". In other words, if you're using an adjective to describe the weather, you'd use *il fait...* before it. However, if you're describing a current weather action, like rain or snow, you use the verb for those: *neiger* and *pleuvoir* specifically. "It's snowing" would be "Il neige" (Il nehj) and "It's raining" would be "Il pleut" (Il ploo).

Another verb that we need to cover is *aller*, which means "to go". You need to understand this verb in order to understand the near future tense later.

Aller - *to go*

Conjugation	Meaning	Pronunciation
Je vais	I go	Juu vey
Tu vas	You go	Too vah
Il/elle/on va	He/she/it/one goes	Il/el/ohn vah
Nous all*ons*	We go	Nooz al-LOHN
Vous allez	You all/you (p.) go	Vooz al-LEY
Ils/elles vont	They go	Il/el vohn

You would use *aller* exactly as you'd expect to. If you're going to a place, you of course would use a preposition to denote it. The preposition is generally à:

Je vais à la bibliothèque. (juu vey-z-ah lah beeb-leeh-oh-tek)

I'm going to the library.

We'll talk more about à in the chapter regarding prepositions, though.

There's one more irregular verb I'm going to specifically hop into in this chapter before we head into the next one about the wonderfully confusing world of French pronunciation: *venir*, or "to come". The cool thing about *venir* is that once you understand it, you understand the verbs which spring from it - *revenir*, meaning "to come back/come again"; *devenir*, meaning "to become"; *souvenir*, meaning "to remember". Here's how you would conjugate *venir* and its derivatives:

Venir - *to come*

Conjugation	Meaning	Pronunciation

Je viens	I come	Juu vee-ahn
Tu viens	You come	Too vee-ahn
Il/elle/on vient	He/she/it/one comes	Il/el/ohn vee-ahn
Nous venons	We come	Noo vuu-nohn
Vous venez	You all/you (p.) come	Voo vuu-ney
Ils/elles viennent	They come	Il/el vee-ehn

Venir is often paired with "de", meaning "from" or "of". Observe:

D'où viens-tu? ("Where are you from?", literally "from where are you coming?")

Je viens des États-Unis. ("I come from the United States.")

There are a few more big verbs, but we'll cover them later on in the book. For now, just try to get some practice with -er, -ir, and -re verbs. I've included some regular -er, -ir, and -re verbs in order to help you get the hang of it through practice and dedication.

insert verbs

Articles

Before we move on to the next chapter, it's absolutely necessary that we cover articles. Articles make up a huge part of French. Every single noun must have an article before it, no exceptions. Well, some exceptions, but they're very few.

What are articles? They're not what you read in the paper or on Facebook, shared by a zealous family member. No, *articles* are the part of speech which refers to the marker for a noun. That is to say, look at the following sentences:

*I eat **some** apples.*

*I eat **the** apples.*

*I eat **an** apple.*

Some, the, and *an* are the markers here, because they tell you the specificity of the thing. *Some* means that you're eating any given apples. *The* implies that you're eating a very specific, previously referenced set of apples. *An* implies that you eat any given apple.

In French, this is expanded upon, much like verb conjugation.

Before we talk about that, we need to talk about *gendered nouns*. Every noun in French has a gender. This doesn't mean that an *apple* is a woman, of course. It's not going to bear your child or anything. The genders of nouns are a totally grammatical separation - a holdover from Vulgar Latin, more or less. The genders are also intrinsic to French. A lot of words would be a lot weirder and a lot of phraseologies would be a lot stranger if gendered nouns were slowly phased out.

The idea of gendered nouns may seem extremely bizarre to an English speaker, and indeed, it can be a little strange at first. None of our nouns have genders. But after practice and dedication, you'll start to learn what makes a noun a certain gender and be able to more or less guess what gender a noun is with some degree of accuracy.

It's important to note that the gender of a noun will correlate to it in subject pronouns, like so:

"*Comment tu l'aimes, la pomme?*" (How do you like the apple?)

"*Elle est un peu acide.*" (It's a tad tart.)

"Apple" is feminine - *la pomme* - and so when we reference it in the sentence following, we have to use the feminine pronoun.

Anyhow, back to the main topic of articles.

Firstly, we have *definite articles*. These correspond to "the". There are four different definite articles:

Le - masculine singular: *Le pont* ("*the bridge*")

La - feminine singular: *La vache* ("*the cow*")

Les - plural: *Les enfants* ("*the children*")

L' - followed by vowel: *L'art* ("*the art*")

You use definite articles when you're talking about a specific instance of something. Basically, in the same way that you'd use "the" in English. You also use it when you're referring to something in a broader sense, where in English we'd normally *drop* the article altogether.

For example, if you wanted to say "I like oranges", you'd use the definite articles - *J'aime les oranges* - where in English we don't use an article at all in that sentence.

After definite articles, we have *partitive* articles. These basically mean "some of" or "any". These are as follows:

Du - masculine singular: *Du vin* ("*some wine*")

De la - feminine singular: *De la pizza* ("some pizza")

Des - plural: *Des framboises* ("some raspberries")

De l' - before vowel: *De l'eau* ("some water")

Generally, partitive articles are used in reference to food or drink.

The last form of article in French is the *indefinite* article. This correlates to "a" or "an" in English. This has two forms:

Un - masculine singular: *Un léon* ("A lion")

Une - feminine singular: *Une langue* ("A language")

That about sums up articles in French. We can go a bit further with them, but that involves the next part, which is...

Negation

Okay, I lied. There's actually one more major thing we have to cover before we go onto the next part. That's the concept of "negation". Negation means simply taking something and then turning it negative. We negative things in English by adding "do not". For example:

"I don't like to walk."

"He doesn't talk."

"We don't look."

You can also negate things in French. You do so by surrounding the verb with *ne pas*. The *ne* indicates a negative statement, where the *pas* means specifically "not".

So to take those sentences we just wrote and translate them:

"Je **n'**aime **pas** marcher." (Juu nehm pah mahr-chey)

"Il **ne** parle **pas**." (Il nuu pahrl pah)

"Nous/on **ne** regardons/regarde **pas**." (Noo/ohn nuu ruu-gahr-dohn/ruu-gahrd pah)

See how that works?

Now, how do articles come into play? Well, if you have a negative statement, it's important to take note that the article will change if you're negating a sentence with partitive or indefinite articles. However, it doesn't change in sentences with definite articles.

Here's a sentence with an indefinite article:

J'ai une plume. (I have a pen.)

And here it is, negated:

Je n'ai pas de plume. (I don't have a pen.)

This change, however, does *not* occur in sentences with definite articles.

*As-tu vu **le** film? (Have you seen the film?)*

*Non, je n'ai vu **le** film. (No, I haven't seen the film.)*

While we're on the topic of negation, there are a few special cases where you *don't* use "ne...pas", and where "pas" actually changes.

These are as follows:

Ne...rien	-	"nothing"
Ne...jamais	-	"never"
Ne...pas encore	-	"not yet"
Ne...plus	-	"not any longer"
Ne...personne	-	"nobody"

So you could use these as follows:

Je ne veux rien. ("I want nothing," or "I don't want anything.")

Il ne le fait pas encore. ("He hasn't done it yet.")

Nous ne sommes contents plus. ("We aren't happy anymore.")

They're a little obtuse to learn and understand at first, but they're not too terribly difficult to grasp once you get the hang of them, and they can make your writing far more expressive, too.

Chapter 2: Pronunciation

French is a beast when it comes to pronunciation. I'm not even going to lie to you, not for a second. The hardest thing when it came to learning French for me, starting out, was listening and speaking. Reading and writing French can be a breeze once you grasp the finer points, but actually making sense of the bizarre syllabary, that's another story entirely. It can be really difficult coming from a language like English to understand all of the nuances of French pronunciation. But luckily, I'm here to try to help you through the major parts.

Liaison

The first topic we're going to cover is *liaison*. This is the idea of connecting sounds. It's part of what makes French such a beautiful and graceful language to listen to.

Somewhere along the line during the development of French, the final pronunciation of letters in words dropped for the most part. However, there are certain locations where these letters can still be heard.

Take, for example, the article *les*. By itself, it's boring - it sounds like "lay", and you don't pronounce the *s*. However, if we put a word with a vowel in front of it, like *éléphants* ("elephants", of course), the *s* in *les* is heard:

J'aime bien les éléphants. (Jehm bee-ahn lay-z-ey-ley-fahn-t)
I really like/quite like the elephants.

This is a super important concept to nail. It can be rather difficult to ascertain and follow through with at first. I remember that when I started out in French, this concept absolutely *floored* me. I had no idea what to do with this or how to apply it. After all, French spellings can often be so weird anyway - how was I supposed to remember when one is supposed to insert a consonant you wouldn't normally hear?

Well, it's a natural fear, and as with most fears, it turned out to be rather unfounded. With time and practice, I found myself to naturally pick up liaison.

There are some very specific cases for liaison, however - and some places you never use it.

Generally, you use liaison if the word preceding the vowel ends in either an *l, t, d, p, s, f, and x*. They generally sound as you'd expect, except for *f* which sounds like a *v*, *d* which sounds like a *t*, and *x* which sounds like an *s*.

There are three kinds of liaison in French: *required*, *forbidden*, and *optional*.

Required liaison exist in many different cases. You *have* to use liaison with these words, there is not an option as to whether you do or not. These words are generally words which are linked in some way or another. You'll use this type of liaison after pronouns (*nous allons*), between a number and a noun (*trois amis*), after prepositions which have only one preposition (*en avance*), after articles (*un orange*), after *est*, after *comment* when asking someone how they're doing (*comment allez-vous?*), between a preceding adjective and its respective noun (*bon homme*), and after monosyllabic adverbs (*très horrible*).

Then, there are *forbidden* liaison. No matter what, you don't use the liaison in these cases. You will never, ever use liaison *before* or *after* somebody's name, after et, before the word *onze* (*J'avais onze ans*), before the word "oui" (*Je lui dis "oui"*), after any sort of plural nouns, before the preposition à, after any sort of singular noun, or before an H wherein you actually *say* the h. (These don't come up often in French, though - the H is *usually* silent.)

Then, there are optional liaisons. These are liaisons which you may or may not say. There is no rule regarding these. These pop up because language is always shifting around and modifying itself throughout time. If you encounter a liaison which is out of the realm of the formerly discussed ones, it's safe to say it's an optional liaison.

French vowels

The next major thing to talk about is the French vowels. These are relatively finite compared to English vowels, but can trip you up if you don't know them. There are also more *exact* vowel sounds because the French alphabet has accents, where the English alphabet does not.

Let's start from the beginning, shall we?

a - pronounced as an "ah"
à - pronounced as an "ah"
â - pronounced as a long "ah"
e - middle of a syllable, like "eh"; end of a syllable, like "uu"
é - pronounced like "ay"
ê - pronounced like "eh"
i - pronounced like "ee"
o - pronounced like "oh"
ô - pronounced like "oh" - denotes where a letter has been dropped in the past.
u - there's no comparable English sound; say "eeh" but then round your lips as though you're saying "ooh". The resulting sound is the French *u*.
y - pronounced like "ee"

Then, there are some really important diphthongs you need to remember.

(A diphthong is a combination of two vowels in order to form a new sound.)

ai - pronounced like "eh"
au - pronounced like "oh"
eau - pronounced like "oh"
ei - pronounced like "eh"
eu - pronounced like "uu"
oeu - pronounced like "uu"
oi - pronounced like "wah"
ou - pronounced like "ooh"

French vowels are easy and relatively simple to understand, so long as you practice. Now onto the consonants.

French consonants

The consonants, you most likely know. Here are the ones which aren't so consistent with English and may trip you up.

c - before an e or an i, it will sound like an s; in any other place, it will sound like the "c" in "cool"
ç - will sound like an s always
ch - will sound like the 'sh' in 'shoe'
g - before an e or an i, it will sound like the *s* in the word "pleasure"; in any other place, it sounds like the English g.
h - normally silent
j - sounds like the French g
qu - sounds like the "c" in "cool"
s - sounds normal if at the beginning, but like a z if in the middle of two vowels.

Using these tips, you should be able to irk out French words with little difficulty.

Chapter 3: Past and Future Tenses

French is a rather easy language to learn, but the hardest thing about it when you're coming from an English speaking background is most certainly its numerous convoluted verb tenses.

There are *at least four* basic French past tenses, and just as many basic French future tenses. You can get away with, at the basic level, knowing just two of the French past tenses, and just two of the French future tenses.

Let's take these one at a time.

Passé composé

Passé composé literally means *compound past*, and is the most common past tense used in French. It's used to reference an action which has been completed at the time of speaking, or at some point in the past. It's a relatively simple tense to form.

The passé composé is made up of two parts: the *auxiliary verb*, and the *past participle*. The auxiliary verb is *normally* avoir, but it can also be être (more on that momentarily). The *past participle* is the past tense form of the word. For example, if "I'm eating" is the present continuous, then "I have eaten" is the past perfect, wherein *have* is the auxiliary verb and *eaten* is the past participle. French works similarly.

So how do you form the past participle? It's simple.

For **-ir** verbs, you drop the **-ir** and replace it with an **-i**. *Finir*, for example, would be *fini*.

For **-er** verbs, you drop the **-er** and replace it with an **-é**. Thus, *manger* would become *mangé*.

For **-re** verbs, you drop the **-re** and replace it with an **-u**. Thus, *vendre* would become *vendu*.

To form the passé composé, all you do is conjugate the auxiliary verb to the person speaking (normally *avoir*), and then get the past participle. So "I have eaten" in French would become "J'ai mangé". "He has sold the strawberries" would be "Il a vendu les fraises".

Simple enough, right? Now the question becomes "when do we use être as opposed to avoir?"

Well, there's actually a system for this: just remember DR. and MRS. VANDERTRAMP. Seriously. That's the mnemonic.

When you're using *intransitive* verbs which indicate either motion (going somewhere) or a change of state (changing in some essential way), you use *être* as your auxiliary verb.

The following are the verbs which will use être:

Devenir - to become something
Rentrer - to enter something again
Monter - to go up something (e.g., stairs)
Rester - to stay
Sortir - to leave, exit, or go out
Venir - to come
Aller - to go somewhere
Naître - to be born to somebody
Descendre - to go down something or descend
Entrer - to enter into something
Retourner - to return to something
Tomber - to fall down or trip
Revenir - to return to something or to come back
Arriver - to arrive to/at something
Mourir - to die
Partir - to leave somewhere

An important thing to note about using être as an auxiliary verb is that you must adjust the passé composé to match the gender and person. So "he left" would be "il est venu", but "she left" would be "elle est venue", and "they left" would be "ils sont venus".

This, however, is not the case when you're using *avoir* as the auxiliary verb. When using *avoir*, the subject and the participle need not agree. The past participle of avoir must, however, agree with the direct object pronoun if it's present before the verb. (More on that momentarily.)

Imparfait

So we talked about the most common French past tense. But there's another incredibly important one that we have yet to cover at all. This tense is known as the *imparfait*. The *imparfait*, or "imperfect", doesn't refer at all to a completed event. Rather, it refers to a given ongoing event or state in the past ("I was happy", "I was young") or a repeated event ("I used to watch..."). This concept doesn't have a direct correlative in English, but the English tense "past continuous" or "past progressive" can certainly get across the same exact point.

The imperfect is simple to form.

For **-er** and **-re** verbs, you just drop the ending and add *-ais, -ais, -ait, -ions, -iez,* or *-aient*.

For **-ir** verbs, you do the same, but you add an "iss" before it.

So for example, if you wanted to say "When I was young, I would play often.", you would say "*Quand j'**étais** jeune, je **jouais** souvent.*"

The imperfect is notoriously difficult to master, but it will come in handy quite often for you, so it's worth teaching anyway.

These are the main cases in which you'd want to use the imperfect over the passé composé:

- Actions or states which occurred often and not just once
- Descriptions of either emotional or physical states: personal feelings, one's age, the given time and weather.
- Any states or actions where the duration is ongoing but unknown.
- Used alongside the passé composé in order to give more depth or information.
- Polite suggestion and wishes - "Pourrais-tu m'aider?" : "Could you help me?" (literally "Would you have the ability to give me help?")
- As part of a conditional clause.

Futur Proche

Futur proche literally means "close future" and refers to events which will most certainly happen, and soon. The futur proche is insanely easy to create. All that you do is combine *aller* (to go) conjugated to the person alongside the infinitive of the verb to be carried out in the near future.

Je vais faire les magasins.
"I'm going to go shopping."

Ils vont jouer au basket.
"They're going to go play basketball."

You can combine this, of course, with dates or times to explicitly state when an action is going to be undertaken.

Vas-tu aller à la librairie demain?
"Are you going to the bookstore tomorrow?"

This is, of course, a very simple tense, but you'll find it incredibly useful. When you're out and about and scratching surface-type conversations with native French speakers, it's unlikely that as a tourist or newcomer, you're going to need to tell them your grand far-future life goals. However, if you need to, that's what the next tense is for.

Futur Simple

The *simple future* tense is, well, simple. It's a very no-nonsense tense that is a little more complicated than the previous tense, and it can be quite easy to sound like you have no idea what you're talking about. However, it's worth learning anyway, because it's a rather common tense.

The futur simple just implies something that will happen at some point in the future. The way that you form it is by taking the *entire infinitive* of a verb as the stem, and then adding -*ai*, -*as*, -*a*, -*ons*, -*ez*, or -*ont* depending upon who is talking. If the verb ends in **-re**, then and only then do you remove something from the verb, taking off the final -e before adding your ending.

Note that some verbs are irregular, such as être and avoir. These have the future stems of *ser-* and *aur-*, respectively.

So let's try this with the verb *chanter*, meaning "to sing". Here's how we'd do it:

Chanter - *to sing, futur simple*

Conjugation	Meaning	Pronunciation
Je chanter*ai*	I will sing	Juu shahn-teh-reh
Tu chanter*as*	You will sing	Too shahn-teh-rah
Il/elle/on chanter*a*	He/she/it/one will sing	Il/el/ohn shahn-teh-rah
Nous chanter*ons*	We will sing	Noo shahn-teh-rohn
Vous chanter*ez*	You all/you (p.) will sing	Voo shahn-teh-rey
Ils/elles chanter*ont*	They will sing	Il/el shahn-teh-rohn

Simple enough, right? The futur simple isn't a terribly difficult tense to use in and of itself, and it's rather easy to set up.

You are halfway done!

Congratulations on making it to the halfway point of the journey. Many try and give up long before even getting to this point, so you are to be congratulated on this. You have shown that you are serious about getting better every day. I am also serious about improving my life, and helping others get better along the way. To do this I need your feedback. Click on the link below and take a moment to let me know how this book has helped you. If you feel there is something missing or something you would like to see differently, I would love to know about it. I want to ensure that as you and I improve, this book continues to improve as well. Thank you for taking the time to ensure that we are all getting the most from each other.

Chapter 4: Questions and Objects

We're going to knock out two seemingly unrelated birds with one very big stone in this chapter. In French, questions and objects actually intertwine in a way. I suppose that they intertwine in any given language, really. In a lot of conversations, you'll be talking about a given subject, and in order to carry on the conversation, you'll find it necessary to ask questions about what the other person is saying. So questions like "When did you see it?" or "How did you get in there?" or "How was it?" will naturally crop up.

That is to say that any budding French conversationalist will need both of these concepts quite handily, and I'm prepared to set you up with them.

Questions

French questions are rather easy. Every question is composed of question words. Much like in English, every proper question has a word which designates *what* exactly we're asking about.

In English, these words are *what, why, how, with whom, who, which, how many*, and *where*.

In French, the words are as follows:

Quoi - What
Quand - When
Pourquoi - Why
Quel(le)(s) - Which
Combien de - How many
Comment - How
Où - Where
Qui - Who
Avec qui - With whom

These, of course, function just like they do in English - they can be parts of normal statements, or they can be used in questions.

If used in questions, there's another phrase you need to know: *est-ce que* (pronounced EST kuu). This literally translate to "is it that?". When combined with other question words, or on its own, it signals that the statement following it is a question.

Est-ce que tu l'aimes?
Do you love him?
(literally "is it [the case] that you love him?")

Où est-ce que tu chantes?
Where do you sing?
(literally "Where is it that you sing?")

This phrase already is powerful, but sometimes you don't want such a clunky phrase. Sometimes, in fact, you can say more with less. This is when inverted questions become the go-to.

And indeed, they're a little familiar to us as English speakers. Think of it this way: let's say you walked into your living room wanting to watch a certain show, but your brother or child was there watching TV, though absentmindedly since they're also playing on their DS and seem mostly preoccupied with that. You want to change the channel. What do you do?

Well, so long as you aren't a barbarian, you'll normally ask something along the lines of:
Are you watching the TV?

Which is an inverted question. What if you just wanted to say that they were watching TV? You would instead say:
You are watching the TV.

So the "you" and the "are" were inverted in order to make the sentence into a question. French questions work similarly to this mechanism.

Let's say the same scenario happened. With the little est-ce que trick we just learned, we might be tempted to say this:
Est-ce que tu regardes la télé?

But we can make this a lot shorter and snappier. We can just invert the question:
Regardes-tu la télé?

This kind of inversion will serve you very well and explain a lot of potentially confusing sentences you'll run into.

Direct object pronouns

This is a really tedious but very necessary lesson to give. We use direct object pronouns *constantly*. Think about it: have you ever been talking about something with a friend, and then you something like "Yeah, I saw them" or "Yeah, I heard it."? The answer, of course, is yes. It would be incredibly monotonous, slightly robotic, and ultimately very creepy if we *didn't* have direct object pronouns. It would feel absolutely unnatural to say the name of something every time we brought it up. Of course, it wouldn't if that were just the way we spoke, but from *our perspective* and speaking *the way we do*, it sounds odd. Besides, it saves time. Replacing a multi-syllable name or phrase with the simple "it" or "them" or "him" saves a lot of time and effort in terms of speaking and writing.

So how do direct object pronouns in French work? Well, I'm assuming that you know how they work in English already.

In French, you correlate the previously mentioned object to the correct direct object pronoun based on perspective (is it first person? second person? third person?) and plurality (singular? plural?). Then you just throw it before the noun. (Notice how I just said "throw *it* before the noun" -- direct object pronouns at work!)

The French direct object pronouns are as follows:
me - first person singular
te - second person singular
le, **la**, **l'** - third person singular
nous - first person plural
vous - second person plural
les - third person plural

So let's say that I wanted to say "I'm giving *it* to Jeffrey." How would I do so?

Well, I first recognize the "direct object". Here, it's *it*. Then I analyze to see which word fits it: *it* refers to a singular third person object, so I'll use the third person singular. Then, we have to figure out the gender of the noun. Let's say we're giving Jeffrey a papaya. This translates to *une papaye*, which is feminine. So it's a feminine third person singular direct object. Perfect. The word is *la*.

So to say "I'm giving it to Jeffrey", knowing "it" is *la*, I just have to translate the rest, and throw the *la* before the verb, like so:

Je la donne à Jeffrey.

Honestly, explaining it makes it sound so much more difficult than it really is. In practice, it's a very easy concept to grasp and there's not a whole lot of genuine difficulty involved in it.

Indirect object pronouns

This is where it gets a bit trickier. There's a huge difference between direct object pronouns and indirect object pronouns. The *direct* object is the object which is directly affected by a given verb. The *indirect* object is the object which receives the brunt of the action of the verb.

The way I like to put it is this: without the *direct object*, there is no *verb*. Full stop. If you throw a ball, you can't *detach* the ball from the concept of *throwing*. Either you're throwing a ball, or there is nothing to be thrown. The same with sending a letter. You can't just *send nothing*. You have to have something to *be* sending. You can absolutely *not* detach the concept of the letter from the notion of *sending*.

However, this is where indirect objects are different. You can detach the indirect object from the rest. The indirect object is non-essential. You can throw a ball without throwing it *to* somebody. You can send a letter without sending it *to* somebody (though it may not go anywhere.) You can do these things *without* the existence of the indirect object. But since the indirect object is *there*, it serves to give context to the verb and the direct object, by giving them an end goal and, indeed, a thing for which and to which they're performed.

The French indirect object pronouns are as follows:

me - *to me*
te - *to you*
lui - *to him/to her*
nous - *to us*
vous - *to you all/to you (f.)*
leur - to them

So let's go back to that sentence from the direct object pronoun section: "I'm giving it to Jeffrey". We ended up getting the following:

Je la donne à Jeffrey.

So how do we get the indirect object pronoun here? We first find the preposition, which will indicate to/for whom or what the action is being performed. The preposition here is à, and the prepositional phrase is "à Jeffrey." Thus, the indirect object is Jeffrey. So that's a third person singular indirect object, and it's gender neutral in the indirect object form, so we can just take *lui* and stick it behind our verb too.

Je la lui donne.

This literally means "I'm giving it to him." Not too shabby, no?

The general rule for placement of direct and indirect object pronouns, when you have both, is that they go in alphabetical order.

Adverbial pronouns

There are a couple of other pronouns you need to be aware of. They are as follows:

y - replaces "there"; also replaces "à" and a noun.

en - replaces either a partitive article and noun ("Je mange des pommes" becomes "J'en mange") or replaces *de* followed by an indefinite article and a noun ("J'ai envie d'une plume" becomes "J'en ai envie") which makes it particularly useful for shortening phrases of verbs which traditionally are followed by de (*se souvenir de* - to be reminded of, *avoir besoin de* - to need, *avoir envie de* - to want, and so on...)

These are called *adverbial pronouns*, and will turn out to be quite useful as you go forward with French. You'll understand the usage of them more as you practice with them and read/hear more and more French.

Ce, cela, celui, and so on

One of the most important French phrases you'll ever encounter is *c'est* (sey). It's somewhat of a catchall. For example, "C'est mon chien !" means "This is/that is/it is my dog!". "Ça, c'est mon ami, [name]" can be used to introduce one friend to another. "Ça, c'est intéressant!" means "That's interesting!". The French have such a love affair with "ça, c'est" that they'll use it places where it really doesn't belong, but you'll figure that out on your own.

C'est is a contraction of the pronoun *ce* and the verb *est*. It means approximately "it is", "this is", or "that is" depending upon the context. "Ce" just means "this" or "that". You can use it before a noun, too, to indicate a specific one. For example, "ce chien" means *this dog*. If you do this, you have to pay attention to your spelling. If it's used before a masculine noun with a vowel, you have to use *cet* instead of *ce*. If it's before a feminine noun, you must use *cette*. If it's before a plural noun, you must use *ces*.

There are some other forms, too. *Ceci* and *cela* are important for you to know - they both mean approximately "this" and "that", but can be used somewhat interchangeably. Cela contracts to the popular *ça*.

Then, there's *celui* and *celle*. *Celle* is the feminine form of *celui*. They both mean "this one" or "that one" dependent upon context, and refer to one of a specific group of different people or things in a given set.

These are important pronouns for you to know just because they're so prolific in French usage.

Chapter 5: Adjectives, Adverbs, Conjunctions, and Prepositions

Before we get to the conversational pillars of French, we need to talk about some major parts of speech.

Adjectives

Adjectives are a huge part of speaking any language. They allow you to describe nouns and objects. French adjectives are relatively easy for the most part. However, their only tricky asset is that the vast majority of them have to match their respective objects which they describe in terms of plurality and gender. This can make for quite a mess when you're newer to French.

Take, for example, the French adjective *joli*, meaning "pretty" or "cute". If I wanted to say "He is pretty", I would say "Il est joli". However, if I wanted to say "she is pretty", I would instead say "Elle est joli*e*". Notice the addition of the *e* to make it feminine.

Depending upon what exactly the adjective is, there are different ways to make one feminine. For example, the vast majority of adjectives can be made feminine simply by the addition of an *-e* to the end of it.

A key difference between English and French adjectives is that French adjectives nearly always go *after* the noun in question, which can really trip you up at first. After a while, it starts to make sense in its own way - after all, it's just another manner of communication. However, avoid falling into the trap of accidentally using an adjective incorrectly because you don't know any better.

Some adjectives *do* go before the noun though. It can be hard to remember which ones exactly, but just think of the following acronym: *beauty, age, goodness, size*. Adjectives which have to do with those typically can go before the adjective rather than after.

Additionally, you very much need to be wary of the meanings of your adjectives. Certain adjectives can go before *and* after a noun. However, this can create two diametrically different meanings depending upon the placement. Take, for example, *curieux*.

If you place *curieux* before the noun, it means weird or strange. However, if you place it after the noun, it means curious or inquisitive. In other words, the correct adjective placement can be the difference between giving praise to your kid and calling them a total weirdo. Be more careful than to call your kid a total weirdo, my friend.

Adverbs

Adverbs describe verbs and adjectives. Adverbs are incredibly easy to form. You may notice a parallel between French adverbs and Spanish adverbs if you've spent any time study Spanish, by chance: you form adverbs by taking the adjective you'd like to make into an adverb, putting it into its feminine form, and appending *ment* to it, similar to how you form adverbs in Spanish.

Take, for example, the adjective *lent*, meaning slow. Now, let's put it in its feminine form, which gives us *lente*. Then, we just add *ment*, the French equivalent of the English "-ly", and we've got *lentement* meaning *slowly*. In a sentence:

"Parleriez-vous lentement? Je ne parle pas bien français." ("Would you speak slowly? I don't speak French well.")

Overall, the process of creating adverbs in French is super easy.

Conjunctions

Conjunctions are an integral part of any language. I say this because we haven't talked about them at all, yet there's not really a part of language which is dedicated to providing logical order to sentences so much as the conjunctions are.

There are quite a few conjunctions in the French language. More than quite a few, actually. There are a ton of them. Let's start with the coordinating conjunctions. What coordinating conjunctions are are conjunctions that serve to connect two different clauses without placing some sort of emphasis on one or the other. In French, there are actually seven different coordinating conjunctions.

Mais - but
Et - and
Ou - or
Or - now
Ni - neither, nor (used in pairs)
Parce que - because
Donc - thus, so

These all have their own particular uses, and you can likely figure out approximately how to use them based off of their English translations. Indeed, basing their usage off of their English translations is a relatively safe way to use these powerful parts of speech.

Next, there are *subordinating* conjunctions. These are a bit more complicated to use, so if something a little weird, I'll put an example by it in parentheses.

Comme - like, as, since (*Il est courageux comme le léon - he is courageous like the lion*)
Quand - when
Lorsque - when
Que - that (*Je sais bien que tu as raison - I know for certain that you're right.*)
Si - if

And then there are just some general ones that you need to know:

Avant que - before the event of (*Je suis parti avant qu'elle est arrivée. - I left before she arrived.*)
Autant que - to the extent that
Bien que - although
Tel(le)(s) que - such that

This is just scratching the surface, really. There are absurd amounts of French conjunctions out there. But with the knowledge that I've given you thus far, you should be able to make your way around moderately well.

Prepositions

We've already learned a couple of prepositions in French, such as à (meaning to, at, or in) and de (meaning of or from). However, there are even more that we haven't talked about! A lot of these things which have relatively direct English translations, but others are ones which will take a bit more explanation. Let's dive in.

à cause de - thanks to (negative)
à travers - through
après - after
au lieu de - instead of something
avant - before
avec - with
chez - *chez* is a tricky one. It can mean "at the location of *x* person's house", where chez moi means "at my home" or "to my home"; it can also mean "at a company's name" as in "J'ai mangé chez McDonald's"; lastly, it can simply mean "for" - "Quel marche chez toi?" meaning "What worked for you?"
contre - against something
dans - in (used if followed by article)
depuis - since, for (in reference to a length of time)
dès - ever since
en - in (used if not followed by article)
entre - between
environ - approximately
grâce à - thanks to (positive)
jusqu'à - up to, until

par - by, before, alongside, through
pendant - during, for (in reference to a length of time)
pour - for
sous - under
sur - on
vers - towards something, but also to say "around" when talking about numbers

    Those are a ton of prepositions to hopefully get you started. You need to be using a lot of this to the extent that you can. Be writing to yourself in private journals and things of the like; try your hand at reading online news and forums. Work with what you've learned.

Chapter 6: Conversational Necessities

So you've landed in France or Quebec and wherever, and you've got a working knowledge of the *mechanics* of French. But *oupsie*, you've got no clue how to have a conversation. What do we do here?

Well, I'll admit, I waited until the last chapter to teach you to have a French conversation because otherwise, you'd just be doing the tourist-y thing of learning several words and phrases without learning *how* they work or *why* they work. And I'll be honest, you'll have a much easier time communicating in France or Quebec if you know how the language works, because the tourist-y phrases hardly make any sense from a linguistic standpoint.

Anyhow, I'll walk you through a French conversation, perhaps with an acquaintance or perhaps with someone new.

The first thing you're going to want to do, of course, is say hello. There are a lot of ways that you can do this in French.

First, if it's in the morning or afternoon, you could say *bonjour*. If it's the evening, you could say *bonsoir*.

This is very formal though. In less formal situations, perhaps around people you know, say *Salut!* instead. (sah-loo) You could also get away with saying *Hé!*

And of course, if you're answering the phone, you say *Allô*. (ah-loh) This is equivalent to the English "hello?" on the phone, and carries the same weight.

If you're wanting to welcome people, you'd say "Bienvenue!". (bee-ahn-vuu-noo)

Anyhow, now you've said hello. What do you do?

Well, you could ask the person a little bit about how they're doing. If they're a stranger, your best bet is to say "Comment allez-vous?" which means "How are you doing?" It's the formal phrase, and can be used with strangers as well as the elderly and your higher-ups in school and work. If you know the person a bit better, you might say "Comment ça va?" (coh-mohn sah vah) or "Comment vas-tu?" (coh-mohn vah tue)

Let's say that you want to get to know them. You may say "Qu'est-ce que tu aimes faire?" or "qu'est-ce que vous aimez faire?" depending upon the formality of the situation, both meaning "What do you like to do?"

Or maybe you're younger and trying to find out how old someone about your age is. In that case, you could just say "Tu as quel âge?", literally meaning

"You have what age?"

Finally, it's going to eventually come to be time to end the conversation, sadly. At that point, there are a couple different ways in which you could say goodbye.

The first is **au revoir**, meaning simply "until we meet again". Pronounced oh ruu-vwah, it's useful in most any situation, formal or informal.

Then, there is **à plus tard** (ah plue tar) which means "see you later", but this is purely informal. You may hear this as "à plus" (ah plues).

Next up is **à bientôt** (ah bee-ehn-toh) which means "see you soon". You can use this formally, as well as informally.

Also useful is **à la prochaine** (ah lah pro-shehn), which means "until next time". Use this when you don't know when you're going to see the other person.

À demain (ah duu-mahn) can mean "see you tomorrow".

Last is **adieu**, which is the most final goodbye. You only use this when you know you'll never see somebody again. If the French hit one nail on the head every time, it's dramaticism.

To spare you from the cheesy explanations from everything, I'm now just going to put some really useful phrases that you're probably going to end up using at one time or another in your journey. I hope the context and background I've given you serves you well in understanding them and there usage:

S'il te plaît/s'il vous plaît - *Please.*
Je voudrais [...] - *I would like [...]*
Je prends [...] - *I'll have [...]*
Merci. - *Thank you.*
Je m'appelle [...] - *My name is [...]*
Comment est [...] - *How is the [...] ? / What's [...] like?*
D'accord. - *Okay.*
Je ne sais pas. - *I don't know.*
Je n'ai aucune idée. - *I have no idea.*
De rien. - *You're welcome.*
Pas de problème. - *No problem.*
Pas de soucis. - *Don't worry.*
Je ne te comprends pas. - *I'm not understanding you.*
Comment dit-on [...] en français? - *How do you say [...] in French?*
Qu'est-ce que ça va dire, [...] ? - *What does [...] mean?*
Combien coûte-t-il? - *How much does it cost?*

Conclusion

Thank for making it through to the end of **Learn French** let's hope it was informative and able to provide you with all of the tools you need to achieve your goals whatever they may be.

The next step is to go further with all of this. I've given you the essential grammatical knowledge, but the trade-off of teaching you so much so briskly is that I didn't give you as much in-depth knowledge regarding vocabulary as I would have liked to. This works out in your favor, though - I encourage you to use Duolingo in order to build your vocabulary. This is because where free online services fail is where I've succeeded. I've tried to give you a firm *grammatical* basis of French, that way when you do learn vocab, you know precisely how to use it. Duolingo and services as such are great for memorizing vocab, but don't do so hot when it comes to giving you the practical knowledge of application.

By using the combination of the two - my technical knowledge of the language and the great reference book I've left you with, and the immense focus of Duolingo on vocabulary, you'll be set straight for success and will have an awe-inspiring grasp of the language in no time.

You can also use the site ankisrs.net in order to put the vocab that you've learned into flash cards. You can use this online flash cards utility in order to hone your ability to speak French like a champion.

I genuinely hope that over the course of this book, I've managed to set you up for success. I fully believe that I have, but the proof will be in the pudding of you learning and applying French in your day to day life. I fully expect that you can do that.

Finally, if you found this book useful in anyway, a review on Amazon is always appreciated!

Enjoy yourself, and every second that you spend learning this beautiful language.

Help me improve this book

While I have never met you, if you made it through this book I know that you are the kind of person that is wanting to get better and is willing to take on tough feedback to get to that point. You and I are cut from the same cloth in that respect. I am always looking to get better and I wish to not just improve myself, but also this book. If you have positive feedback, please take the time to leave a review. It will help other find this book and it can help change a life in the same way that it changed yours. If you have constructive feedback, please also leave a review. It will help me better understand what you, the reader, need to make significant improvements in your life. I will take your feedback and use it to improve this book so that it can become more powerful and beneficial to all those who encounter it.

REMEMBER TO JOIN THE GROUP NOW!

If you have not joined the Mastermind Self Development group yet, now is your time! You will receive videos and articles from top authorities in self development as well as a special group only offers on new books and training programs. There will also be a monthly member only draw that gives you a chance to win any book from your Kindle wish list!

If you sign up through this link
http://www.mastermindselfdevelopment.com/specialreport you will also get a special free report on the Wheel of Life. This report will give you a visual look at your current life and then take you through a series of exercises that will help you plan what your perfect life looks like. The workbook does not end there; we then take you through a process to help you plan how to achieve that perfect life. The process is very powerful and has the potential to change your life forever. Join the group now and start to change your life!
http://www.mastermindselfdevelopment.com/specialreport

You will also love these other great titles from Mastermind Self Development!

You will want to check out these other great titles Mastermind Self Development. All available in the Kindle store or you can just click on covers below.

http://viewbook.at/selflove

http://mybook.to/positivethink

You can also find these titles by searching them in the Kindle store on Amazon.

www.ingramcontent.com/pod-product-compliance
Lightning Source LLC
Chambersburg PA
CBHW081409070526
44583CB00020B/2742